Indiana Pacers

Richard Rambeck

CREATIVE ● EDUCATION

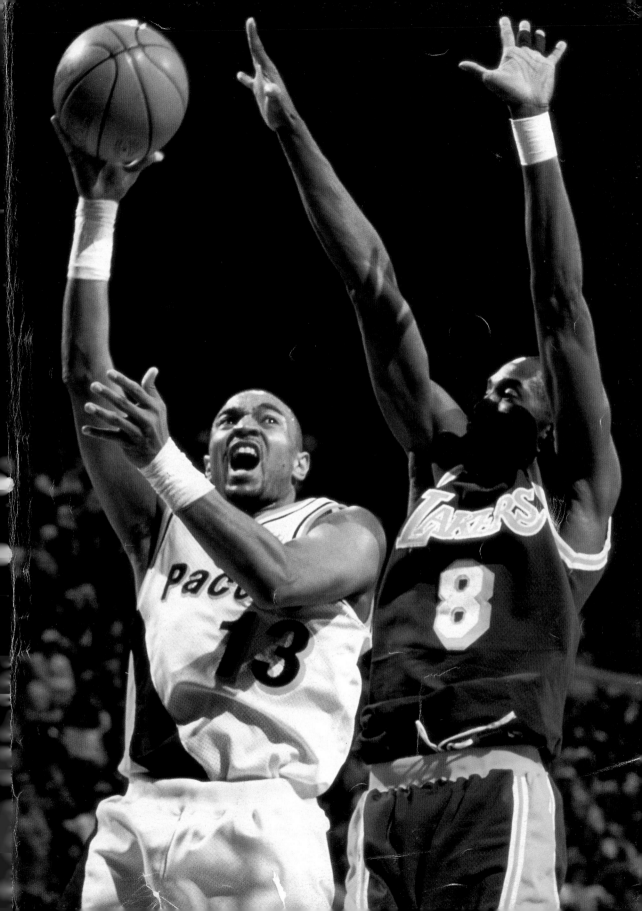

Published by Creative Education
123 South Broad Street, Mankato, Minnesota 56001
Creative Education is an imprint of The Creative Company

Designed by Rita Marshall

Photos by: Allsport Photography, NBA Photos, UPI/Corbis Bettmann, and
SportsChrome.

Photo page 1: Rik Smits
Photo title page: Mark Jackson

Library of Congress Cataloging-in-Publication Data

Rambeck, Richard.
Indiana Pacers / Richard Rambeck.
p. cm. -– (NBA today)
Summary: Describes the background and history of the Indiana Pacers
pro basketball team.
ISBN 0-88682-876-7

1. Indiana Pacers (Basketball team)—History—Juvenile literature.
[1. Indiana Pacers (Basketball team)—History. 2. Basketball—History.]
I. Title. II. Series: NBA today (Mankato, Minn.)

GV885.52.I53R36 1997   96-6533
796.323'64'09772—dc21

First edition

5 4 3

Indiana is located in the heart of the Midwest. It is fairly close to Chicago and Detroit, as well as many major cities in the eastern United States. Indiana, with a diverse economy centered on strong manufacturing and agricultural industries, calls itself the "Crossroads of America." Most of the population is found in the northern part of the state, where heavy manufacturing thrives. In the central and southern parts of Indiana, farmlands dominate the rolling hills and fertile plains.

Residents of Indiana are nicknamed "Hoosiers." They

The original Pacer, Roger Brown.

Freddie Lewis led Indiana in scoring during the team's first ABA season.

have a great love of sports, particularly basketball. In fact, basketball hoops are almost as common on the farms and in the small towns of Indiana as they are on the concrete playgrounds of most major cities. The love of basketball binds Indiana residents together, whether they are urban or rural. This devotion to basketball was illustrated several years ago in a movie called *Hoosiers,* which was based on a true story about a small-town high school team that won the state basketball championship.

In that movie, the small-town team played the finals in Indianapolis, which is the state capital and largest city in Indiana. Indianapolis is also home to the National Basketball Association (NBA) franchise known as the Indiana Pacers. The team was formed in 1967 as one of the original members of the American Basketball Association (ABA), which merged with the NBA in 1976.

Since 1976, the NBA Pacers have struggled to win games and to live up to the expectations of their basketball-crazy Indiana fans. In the 1990s the Pacers have finally established a winning pace. Behind the talents of such players as Erick Dampier and Reggie Miller, and with a new coach, former Celtics great Larry Bird, they are looking to bring an NBA crown to the state where basketball is king.

PACERS SET THE PACE IN THE ABA

When the ABA's Indiana Pacers were first formed, the team's owners weren't sure that the Indianapolis area was ready to support pro basketball. General manager Mike Storen knew that the state's many basketball fans would

Antonio Davis, a top rebounder off the bench.

Mel Daniels set all-time ABA Pacers records for shots taken (38) and made (25).

only come out to see an exciting, winning team. Storen set out to put that type of club together. After a so-so first season in 1967–68, Storen brought in a new coach, Bob "Slick" Leonard, and then tried to build a team around high-scoring forward Roger Brown.

Storen traded for the rights to two players who would have big roles in making the Pacers a winning team: 6-foot-9 center Mel Daniels and high-scoring forward Bob Netolicky. Daniels became one of the dominant centers in the ABA. The 230-pounder won the league's Most Valuable Player award in 1968–69, averaging 24 points and almost 17 rebounds a game. Netolicky joined with Roger Brown in the Pacers frontcourt. Together, the two forwards averaged nearly 40 points per game.

While Daniels, Brown, and Netolicky looked good on the court, "Slick" Leonard was known for how he looked off the court. The coach earned his nickname because he was such a sharp dresser. He would show up for the games wearing expensive suits. Once play started, however, his outfits would soon become rumpled and sweat-stained. Leonard was a fiery, intense coach who demanded total dedication from his players. On the sidelines, he would pace constantly, turn pirouettes, and scream at referees.

Whatever Leonard did, it worked. The Pacers made it to the league championship series in both 1968–69 and 1969–70, winning the 1969–70 ABA title.

Leonard's boss, Mike Storen, eventually left the Pacers to become commissioner of the ABA. But before he left, Storen made one more move that would assure the Pacers a place at the top of the league for several years to come. Storen was looking for a player who could dominate a game with his strength, and he didn't have to go very far to find the "Baby Bull" he was seeking. That was the nickname of George McGinnis, a 6-foot-8, 235-pound package of muscles who was playing for Indiana University.

1 9 7 2

Darnell Hillman's 10 blocks against Florida established a team record.

During Indiana University's 1970–71 season, McGinnis led the Big Ten in scoring with a 29.9 average. He also grabbed 14.4 rebounds a game. McGinnis was only a sophomore, but he wasn't really interested in finishing his college career. Storen knew that Big George wanted to turn pro, so he offered McGinnis a $50,000 bonus if the college star would sign with the Pacers. At least two NBA teams—Chicago and Phoenix—also wanted McGinnis. But the Baby Bull, who had grown up in Indiana, wanted to stay close to home.

"It may sound square," McGinnis explained, "but I'm basically a country boy. I don't like big cities. Indianapolis is a clean, friendly place. It's got a small-town atmosphere." Thanks to McGinnis's decision to sign with Indiana, the Pacers now had a big-time star. McGinnis helped the powerful Pacers roll to the 1971–72 ABA title. They literally shoved their opponents aside on the way to a championship.

"Yeah," said a grinning George McGinnis after the season ended, "I like the pro game. I like the physical contact. I like

The dominating George McGinnis.

In the early 1990s, George McCloud intimidated opponents. 11

going inside, knocking a few people around and coming out with the ball."

George might have liked physical play, but opponents on other ABA teams hated going up against the rugged Pacer forward. "McGinnis is so strong you'd swear he weighs 300 pounds," claimed Virginia Squires forward Willie Wise. "When he posts inside on you, there's nothing you can do. He's going to the basket."

Roger Brown proved his durability by becoming the first ABA star to play in 500 games.

McGinnis went to the basket enough times during the 1972–73 season to help lead the Pacers to their third league title in five years. In the ABA championship series, Indiana defeated the Kentucky Colonels in a hard-fought seven-game battle. "Man," said an ecstatic McGinnis after the final game, "I'm just a kid. Only 22, and I've already got two championships. Now that's something, isn't it."

Unfortunately for the Pacers and their loyal fans, the team's success would soon end. Many of Indiana's stars, including Mel Daniels and Roger Brown, had gotten older and weren't as effective as they had been earlier in their careers. McGinnis remained one of the top players in the league, but his team started to slip in the standings.

After the 1974–75 season, it was obvious that ABA teams wouldn't be able to keep their best players from jumping to the richer, more stable NBA. One of those players was George McGinnis, who signed a multimillion-dollar contract with the Philadelphia 76ers. McGinnis didn't really want to leave his home state, but he knew that the money was too good to pass up.

A year after McGinnis left the Pacers, the ABA and NBA merged. The Pacers, Denver Nuggets, New York Nets, and

San Antonio Spurs all became NBA teams. Denver and San Antonio both had fine young teams that would have immediate success in the older league. The Nets struggled after losing Julius Erving to the Philadelphia 76ers. And the Pacers? Coach Bob Leonard knew he needed to rebuild the club. All the stars from Indiana's three ABA championship teams had retired or moved on to other teams. Leonard had only two weapons he could count on—high-scoring forward Billy Knight and Don Buse, a smooth guard with lightning-quick hands on defense.

1 9 7 6

During the ABA's last season, Don Buse recorded 346 steals, the most in pro basketball.

BUSE STEALS THE HEARTS OF INDIANA FANS

Don Buse had been a big offensive star in college at Evansville, but the Pacers wanted him to do other things. It was Buse's job to control Indiana's offense and get the ball to such scorers as Billy Knight. It was also his job to use his quick hands to disrupt the other team's offense. Don Buse's effectiveness on the court was measured in the numbers of assists and steals he recorded. In the Pacers' first season in the NBA, Buse led the league in both statistics—with 685 assists and 281 steals. He also paved the way for Knight to become one of the top scorers in the league, with an average of more than 25 points a game.

"It's because of Buse that I'm having a great year," Knight explained. "I'll pass the ball in and he'll be bringing it up. He'll ask me if there's anything special I want to run. I tell him I'll do something, then I do it, and the ball comes right to me."

Coach Bob Leonard appreciated Buse as much as Knight

Dudley Bradley recorded an NBA high for the most steals (211) in a rookie season.

did. "He is as consistent a player as I've ever seen," Leonard observed. "How well we do usually just depends on how the other players do around him."

Not many NBA fans outside of Indianapolis knew about Don Buse. In fact, a lot of the players in the league weren't sure who he was. But the coaches knew all about Buse. "He's a superb ball handler, and he's unselfish," said Chicago Bulls assistant coach Jerry Sloan. "His game is helping other people, and there are a lot of teams that are starving for a player like that."

Despite the play of Buse and Knight, however, the Pacers were starved for victories during the late 1970s. After being the best team in the old ABA, the Pacers were unable to even make the playoffs in the NBA. As a result, "Slick" Leonard lost his job after the 1979–80 season. The Pacers fired the man who had coached them for a dozen years and led them to three championships.

New coach Jack McKinney brought a different system and a new attitude to Indiana. Under McKinney, the Pacers would try to outthink their opponents. McKinney's new system enabled the Pacers to reach a goal that Leonard had been unable to help them achieve—they became contenders in the NBA playoffs. Indiana finished the 1980–81 season with a 44–38 record, and Jack McKinney was named NBA Coach of the Year. Even though the Pacers were swept by Philadelphia in the first round of the playoffs, hopes were high for the future.

Those hopes, however, were dashed by bad luck and inconsistency. McKinney coached until 1984, but was unable to produce another winning team. The club did draft two

14   *High-scoring Billy Knight.*

The versatile Herb Williams.

outstanding young forwards during McKinney's reign—Herb Williams and Clark Kellogg—who became the cornerstones of the team. But such players as Don Buse, guard Johnny Davis, and forward Louis Orr were lost to the free-agent market. As a result, Indiana finished with the worst record in the Eastern Conference in both 1982–83 and 1984–85.

After both of those seasons, the Pacers had a shot at the number one pick in the NBA draft. Both times, however, they lost the coin toss or lottery and wound up with the second choice—and second best wasn't quite good enough to build a great team. Indiana missed out on getting the talents of centers Ralph Sampson, who was taken by Houston in 1983, and Patrick Ewing, who was drafted by the New York Knicks in 1985. The Pacers were able to grab fine players both years—center Steven Stipanovich and forward Wayman Tisdale. But neither was able to turn the franchise around.

1 9 8 5

Jerry Sichting led the team in assists and free-throw percentage for the third straight year.

PACERS FIND THE RIGHT PERSON IN THE DRAFT

In 1986, the Pacers finally hit the jackpot in the college draft, selecting 6-foot-8 forward Chuck Person from Auburn University. At first Indiana fans booed the choice of Person. Most of them had not heard of him. "I would have booed, too," Person admitted. "But don't make snap judgments until you see me play. If you like basketball, you'll love Chuck Person."

At Auburn, Person had played in the shadow of teammate Charles Barkley, who left school after his junior year to turn pro. Person stayed at Auburn for the full four years and became the leading scorer in school history. Auburn coach

Outstanding Pacers draft pick Chuck Person, left (pages 18–19).   17

Rookie Wayman Tisdale's .515 field-goal percentage led the Pacers.

Sonny Smith called Person "the most complete player I've ever coached." Person was confident, and he didn't mind telling fans and opposing players how good he was. Person also had a huge grin on his face most of the time. "A smile and a handshake go a long way in life," the personable Person explained.

Chuck Person did more than smile and shake hands during his first season in Indiana. He used his deadly long-range jump to lead the team in scoring with an 18.8 average, and was Indiana's second-leading rebounder. He was named NBA Rookie of the Year following the 1986–87 season. Person also gained the respect of the rest of the players in the league, including Boston Celtics star Larry Bird.

During one game in his rookie season, Person was getting frustrated at his inability to stop Bird. At one point the

Clark Kellogg, a scoring and rebounding leader.

Celtics star turned to Person and said, "Don't be discouraged. You're a great player. Julius Erving did the same thing to me when I first came into the league."

Person might have gotten down on himself occasionally, but he never stopped believing he could do the job. "He has loads of confidence," said Boston Celtics coach K.C. Jones. "And that's what you need if you want to be called great." That's exactly what Person wanted to be called: "One of these days," he predicted, "I'm going to achieve greatness."

Defensive ace Steve Stipanovich had 106 steals to top all NBA centers.

Person's trademark was his jump shot. His powerful arms enabled him to launch long-range bombs with a minimal amount of motion. Teammates called the long-shooting Person "the Rifleman." In fact, Person was actually named for a rifleman. His mother had named him Chuck Connors Person after actor Chuck Connors, who played the title role in a 1960s television show called *The Rifleman*.

During the 1986–87 season, Person had enough shots to help new Indiana coach Jack Ramsay lead the Pacers to the playoffs for the first time in six years. Indiana lost to Atlanta, but Hoosier fans were sure that the future held great promise for their favorite team.

REGGIE FINDS HIS RANGE IN INDIANA

Unfortunately, the Pacers' bright future was soon clouded by injuries to starting forward Clark Kellogg and center Steve Stipanovich. Both players were forced to retire. Luckily, these setbacks were balanced by the selection of Reggie Miller in the 1987 NBA draft. Miller, a great outside

21

22

NBA All-Star Reggie Miller.

scorer, would soon become one of the best pure shooters ever to play in the NBA.

While Miller may have been second to none as an NBA shooter, he still played in the huge shadow cast by one of his siblings—his sister Cheryl, perhaps the greatest woman basketball player in history. Cheryl Miller went to the University of Southern California in Los Angeles and led the Trojans to two national championships. Reggie, a couple of years younger than Cheryl, went to UCLA. The joke was that Reggie was the only player on the UCLA team who couldn't outplay his sister. At one time, that was true.

Vern Fleming's three triple-doubles established him as one of the NBA's best guards.

"I woke Reggie one day and asked him if he was ready for another beating," Cheryl Miller said, recalling a day when both were teenagers. "When he got up, he kept getting up. And up and up. All of a sudden, he was 6-foot-6. We went outside for our usual head-to-head game. I took first outs, blew by him like always, and sailed in for the layup. As I was running under the basket, I heard this noise. Clang. I looked up, and the ball was still there. So was Reggie. He had pinned it against the backboard. I stopped in my tracks. 'Uh, Reg,' I said. 'How about a game of HORSE?'"

Reggie Miller probably could have beaten almost anybody at HORSE because of his ability to hit jump shots from 30 to 35 feet from the basket. He would often launch NBA-style three-point bombs while in college, several feet beyond the college three-point line, which was 19 feet, 9 inches from the basket. Most pro scouts figured Miller would have no trouble adjusting to the pro game and its three-point line, which was four feet farther out than the college line.

Despite his outside shooting ability, Miller struggled during his rookie year with the Pacers, but he soon blossomed into a young star. He was the second-leading scorer for Indiana—behind Person—during the 1988–89 season. The Pacers, however, stumbled to a 28–54 record, which placed them last in the NBA's Central Division. As a result, Jack Ramsay was replaced as coach by Dick Versace, who vowed to make the Pacers a consistent, winning team.

Second-year player Scott Skiles's free-throw percentage of .903 led the NBA.

The team Versace took over was talented, but unpredictable. Indiana had made several trades, so most of the players were new to the team. Forward Detlef Schrempf came from Dallas in the trade of Herb Williams. Forward LaSalle Thompson came from Sacramento in exchange for Wayman Tisdale. Forward Mike Sanders came from the Cleveland Cavaliers, and 7-foot-4 center Rik Smits was drafted out of tiny Marist College. The only holdovers were Chuck Person, Reggie Miller, and Vern Fleming.

In 1989–90, led by Miller—who scored almost 25 points a game—and Person, the Pacers posted their first winning season in nine years. Indiana finished 42–40 and earned the right to play defending NBA champion Detroit in the first round of the 1990 playoffs. The Pacers played hard, but they were no match for the powerful Pistons, who went on to win their second straight title.

MOVING AHEAD IN THE 1990S

Following their early exit from the 1990 playoffs, the Pacers were determined to go farther the next year. Unfortunately, the 1990–91 season started badly for the team. By early January, the Pacers had one of the worst records in the

NBA. Versace was fired as coach and replaced by assistant Bob Hill, who had previously served a brief stint as head coach of the New York Knicks. The coaching change worked, and the Pacers started to win. They ended up making the playoffs for the second straight season.

At 7-foot-4, Rik Smits recorded more than 150 blocks for a second straight year.

As usual, Miller and Person led the way, but they had plenty of help this time. Detlef Schrempf came off the bench and provided instant offense and solid defense. He was named the NBA's Sixth Man of the Year. Schrempf was probably Indiana's most versatile player—he could shoot, pass, rebound, and play tough defense. In addition, young center Rik Smits successfully battled injuries and showed signs of becoming one of the best young pivotmen in the game.

In the 1991 playoffs, the young Pacers battled the powerful Boston Celtics point for point. The two teams split the first four games of the series, setting up a do-or-die fifth contest in Boston Garden. Despite trailing 110–96 with seven minutes left, the Pacers refused to die. Person hit one three-pointer, then another, and another. Miller, too, dropped a long-range bomb.

Suddenly Boston's lead was only 120–118 with 22 seconds left. After a Celtic turnover, the Pacers got the ball to Person, who had already made 17 of 31 three-point shots in the series. He had the ball on the left side of the court. He could have tried to drive inside for the tying basket, but he wasn't about to settle for a tie. He jumped and shot his patented three-pointer. This time, though, the Rifleman missed the target by the smallest of margins. And the Celtics held on to win, just barely.

In the locker room after the game, a weary Chuck Person

Mark Jackson, an NBA leader in assists (pages 26-27).

slipped out of his sweaty uniform. "They got us that time," Person muttered. "But we'll be back."

"Super sub" Detlef Schrempf led the Pacers in rebounds for the second straight year.

MILLER ON THE MARK

Person was right; the Pacers were back in the playoffs throughout the 1990s. Though they were one of the NBA's better teams, the Pacers continued to lose to various teams in the playoffs. So changes came to Indiana. Person was traded to the Minnesota Timberwolves and Schrempf was dealt to the Seattle SuperSonics. Indiana also brought in Larry Brown in 1994 to coach the Pacers.

Brown had a reputation as a winner. As a college coach, he won NCAA championships at UCLA and Kansas. As a pro, he was ABA Coach of the Year three times, and came to the Pacers with nearly 500 victories in the NBA. In a coaching career spanning nearly 25 years, Brown's teams had only suffered one losing season.

"He wins immediately," said Pacers president Donnie Walsh, Brown's long-time friend. "Larry comes in and wins immediately with what you've got, and to me that's what a really good coach is."

In his first three years as the Pacers coach, Brown led the club to two seasons in which the Pacers won over 50 games—a feat Indiana hadn't accomplished since the early 1970s in the ABA. Brown relied on All-Star Reggie Miller for continuity. By the start of the 1996–97 season, Miller had logged more playing minutes than any Pacer in history, and he was the only Pacer selected to play on more than one All-Star team. He was chosen to play on Dream Team II and also in the Olympic Games on the U.S. Dream Team III, starring in the team's gold-medal run. Miller, one of the most prolific three-point shooters in NBA history, also carried with him a reputation as a trash-talker on the court.

But Miller cemented his reputation as an NBA superstar in game five of the 1994 Eastern Conference Finals against the Knicks. Miller had one of the best performances in NBA playoff history, scoring 25 points in the fourth quarter, including a record five three-pointers in the fourth period, and six three-pointers in the second half of the game, which tied another record—all in a Pacers victory.

1 9 9 6

Coach Larry Brown won his 500th NBA game and became the Pacers' all-time winningest coach.

"A few seconds can be an eternity," said Miller about his performance. "We're down six. Then I hit a three. Then I see Anthony Mason inbounding the ball, losing control, and I intercept. I think, 'We're on the road. Let's go for the jugular.' So I step back for the three. Tie game."

Though the Pacers lost the next two games and eventually the series, Miller and his club got their revenge against the Knicks in the 1995 Eastern Conference Semifinals, in which Miller scored eight points in less than nine seconds, keying a Pacers come-from-behind victory. The Pacers won the series against the Knicks, but lost in the Conference Finals to the Orlando Magic.

Miller wasn't done proving his worth to the Pacers. After suffering a fractured eye socket late in the 1995–96 season, Miller made a dramatic comeback in front of the Indiana home crowd in the last game of a first-round playoff series against the Atlanta Hawks. Though Miller scored 29 points, the Hawks won the game by two points, eliminating Indiana.

Before the 1996–97 season—a year in which the Pacers

All-Star Dale Davis.

Agile center Erick Dampier.

Travis Best tallied a career-high 11 assists in a victory over the Hornets.

looked like a team building for the future—Miller spoke of the previous season: "I thought we could get to the next round, but it wasn't to be. When I got in there, my vision was only about 75 percent. It was fuzzy. Now," he gauged, "it's 100 percent again and I'm ready to go."

The Pacers are counting on their young players to improve and carry them into the future. "We were a very old team, and now we're one of the youngest," said Brown. "And not only young, but a team with a chance to get better. Travis Best, I think, is going to play a significant role. Jalen Rose is going to play a significant role. I think Erick Dampier is going to have a chance to be a star in this league."

But with their 1996–97 record hovering just under .500, the Pacers decided they needed more veteran leadership— and they got it. On February 21, the trading deadline date, Denver Nuggets point guard Mark Jackson and center LaSalle Thompson returned to Indiana, the team that had traded them away in the off-season. Jackson was leading the NBA in assists at the time of the trade, and Thompson, with 15 years of experience, was expected to complement and teach Dampier. Everything seemed in place until Pacers management told Larry Brown he was free to leave, which he did. Uncertainty shook the team. Then former Boston Celtics great Larry Bird took Brown's place at the helm. Although it marks Bird's first coaching job, he has a wealth of knowledge and experience to bring to the position. With Bird now in place, the Pacers are more ready than ever to take flight into a promising future.